ANGEL NUMBERS
COLORING BOOK

Discover the Wisdom of Numerology

ANJALI SINGH

DOVER PUBLICATIONS
Garden City, New York

Copyright © 2025 by Michael O'Mara Books Limited
All rights reserved. No part of this publication may be reproduced, downloaded, distributed, transmitted, or stored in any form or by any means, electronic or mechanical, without prior written permission from the publisher.

This Dover edition, first published in 2025, is a slightly modified republication of the work, originally published by LOM Art, an imprint of Michael O'Mara Books Limited, London, in 2025. The text has been edited for an American audience.
  The advice and strategies contained herein may not be suitable for every situation. The publisher does not accept any legal responsibility for any personal injury or other damage or loss resulting from the use of the information in this book.

ISBN-13: 978-0-486-85444-1
ISBN-10: 0-486-85444-2

Edited by Jocelyn Norbury
Written by Imogen Currell-Williams, Bryony Davies, and Jocelyn Norbury
Design by Jade Moore and Moesha Kellaway
Cover design by Angie Allison
Editorial consultancy by MaKayla McRae

Printed in China
85444201   2025
www.doverpublications.com

Introduction

Numbers are all around us. They often go unnoticed, but there are occasions when numerical sequences might catch your eye. These numbers, known as angel numbers, may be messages from a spiritual universe. They can offer divine guidance and hold profound significance in your life.

Discover the hidden meanings of these powerful signs as you color the pages of this book. Familiarize yourself with different types of angel numbers, and unlock their divine wisdom as you explore this unique, ancient, and fascinating art.

Angel numbers are sequences of numbers that are believed to carry special spiritual significance and messages from the divine realm. These numbers often appear repeatedly in everyday life, and each has a specific meaning—providing guidance, reassurance, or a call to action.

Angel number 101

Just as the tiger possesses ferocity and abundant lifeforce, angel number 101 signifies that you are surrounded by great potential. This number encourages you to harness it.

Change and new experiences are the key to growth. Like a tiger is unafraid of predators, you should tackle opportunities head-on, no matter how daunting they seem.

An extraordinary life will inevitably lead you on a path to self-discovery. In return for pursuing your goals fearlessly, you are offered the opportunity for spiritual growth and fulfillment—the ultimate aim for all existence.

Angel number 111

Representing opportunity, good luck, and achievement, angel number 111 celebrates individuality and signals that a fresh start is on the horizon.

A powerful combination of the number 1 (which denotes intuition, independence, and individual power) and master number 11 (signifying the discovery of a higher purpose), angel number 111 offers a clean slate to write the story of your life as you wish. Take a deep breath, believe in yourself and the wisdom of your spirit guide, and manifest your dreams intentionally.

Angel number 123

It is time to move forward with your life. Angel number 123 is an encouraging sign from the universe that good things are imminent, and you should embrace the natural changes that come your way.

It is time to embrace the positive energy around you and use it as a guiding force, showing you the way through the treacherous mountains along the path of success. Go toward the sun. Let go of fear and self-doubt—take inspiration from the mountain goat, which is sure-footed through difficult terrain.

Cacti and succulents signify resilience. They adapt and flourish in tough environments. Relinquish your worries and take steps forward along your chosen path. Angel number 123 reassures you that the universe is on your side.

Angel number 222

A peaceful symbol of balanced and harmonious relationships, angel number 222 encourages you to focus your energy on strengthening existing partnerships. Roses and peonies symbolize equilibrium. This angel number draws attention to areas in your life that are not balanced.

In the natural world, the cycle of life relies on all elements working together. Similarly, if your relationships feel off-kilter, this number reminds you that you can shift interpersonal dynamics through communication and compromise.

Angel number 234

Angel number 234 is a powerful message from the universe, symbolizing growth, balance, and trusting the process. The sequence combines the energies of 2, 3, and 4, representing harmony, creativity, and stability.

When you encounter this number, remember to embrace the natural timing and rhythm of your journey, instead of rushing to reach your final destination. Like the seasons, all of life's transitions are inevitable and important in their own right. By maintaining a positive, patient mindset, you will manifest your desires.

Angel number 234 reassures you that your efforts are supported by divine forces, urging you to keep moving forward with unwavering faith and confidence.

Angel number 333

A beautiful china cup sits atop a pile of books that are embossed with the number 333. If you come into contact with this number, it is time to embrace personal development. Turn your plans into actions—be creative and express yourself. Grab your notebook and pens, and give voice to your inner feelings.

The power of the lucky number 3 is magnified threefold in this angel number. This good fortune and growth are represented by the plants and flowers, especially the money plant. It's a time for growth. Perhaps you might be the one to expand, or you could help others do so. Wholeheartedly invest your best efforts to reach ideal outcomes. The sky's the limit! This advancement could be spiritual, personal, or financial. However it manifests, if you are channeling your energy and love, your desires will flourish. Embrace the empowerment the universe is offering.

Angel number 369

A powerful message from the universe, angel number 369 conveys that your dreams are within reach. The number 3 is associated with self-expression and creativity, while the number 6 signifies home and gratitude. Combined with the spiritual enlightenment that the number 9 represents, this angel number is a sign that you have the power to change your life.

When these three numbers appear together, your creative energy and spiritual growth are in perfect harmony, enabling you to manifest your future and bring it to reality.

Angel number 444

An angel number with protection and support as its central message, 444 is a sign that you are in the hands of a spiritual guide with your best interests at heart. As loyal and unwavering as "man's best friend," your guardian offers protection and encouragement, steering you along the correct course.

Just as irises and snapdragons represent hope and positivity in the face of adversity, angel number 444 offers an optimistic outlook. Although there will be challenges as you travel along life's path, do not be discouraged. Instead, focus on how the reward of achievement will outweigh any hardship.

The warmth and light from the sunrays offer a reminder that you are not alone. There is support to help you through difficult times.

Angel number 555

As a powerful harbinger of transformation and fresh starts, angel number 555 has a lot in common with the fleeting beauty of cherry blossoms in the spring. Just as these flowers bloom briefly but brilliantly, the appearance of 555 suggests that significant changes are on the horizon and, with them, the opportunity for swift renewal and growth.

Angel number 555 encourages you to make peace with times of transition, trusting that they will lead to a brighter, more fulfilling path. The cherry blossom's delicate petals remind you to appreciate the present moment, as change is inevitable and necessary.

Just as the blossoms fall to make way for new growth, 555 signals that it's time to let go of old patterns and make way for fruitful, prosperous seasons ahead.

Angel number 666

If you encounter master number 666, you are probably experiencing a time of imbalance in your life. Some people fear the number, but as it is related to the core numerology of 6, it can bring love, compassion, and healing. Therefore, any imbalance you are sensing can be reconciled with this healing intention.

There are flames near the numbers, but far from being a force for destruction, the fire has a cleansing and restoring power. Fireflies light up the darkness, promising to guide you and provide illumination in times of uncertainty. Luna moths, symbols of spiritual guidance, flutter in the night sky, drawn to the fire's light.

Angel number 777

Get ready. Something wonderful is about to happen! If you encounter angel number 777, it means luck is coming your way. This could be a spiritual awakening bringing a sense of completeness or the manifestation of something you have been waiting for. The angel number is shown on playing cards, emphasizing the great things approaching. Success is portrayed through the lucky charms on the bracelet and the alliums, which symbolize good fortune.

Circular rings and bracelets represent completeness. This angel number will lead to healing and truth. With integrity and transparency come motivation and action, so take heed.

Angel number 818

Take this number as a sign from your angels that positive change is on the horizon. The dawn Sun is rising, bringing with it a new day and a fresh perspective, abundant with energy and spirit.

Just as angel number 818 represents new beginnings, so do the flowers in bloom, symbolizing rebirth while opening themselves up to the Sun to absorb the light. You, too, must open yourself to the world around you, soaking up resourceful energy and harnessing its power.

8 is one of the most divine numbers. Visually similar to the symbol for infinity, it connects you to the spiritual universe and allows you to home in on your own infinite growth.

Angel number 888

The number 8 is replete with positive associations, so it is no surprise that angel number 888 is seen as a gateway to good fortune. If you find this number jumping out at you, take it as a reminder to be open to the gifts that life has to offer. Wealth and success are in your future, and this is a sign that you are on the right path to receive your destiny.

The bounty that awaits is represented by loaded grapevines. A traditional symbol of abundance, they are accompanied by ripe pomegranates. This depicts the "fruits of your labor" and a reinforcement of the idea that good times are coming, in abundance. Bluebirds, associated with hope and positivity, assure you that happiness is on the way. Meanwhile, peonies indicate that material wealth will play a key role in your joy.

Those who manifest this number can prepare themselves for the sweet rewards of their hard work.

Angel number 911

If you come across angel number 911, be prepared for monumental change. The number 9 is the final angel number, which means that a chapter is coming to a close. But don't be alarmed; when one door closes, another opens. The next chapter presents you with an opportunity for growth, courage, and enlightenment.

The number 911 is often used in emergency situations, so be aware of any red flags. Prepare to make bold decisions to prevent having negative energies enter your realm. Just like a worldly cat, use your intuition when responding. As long as you are true to yourself, you will be able to navigate whatever comes your way.

Angel number 999

Now is an opportune time to celebrate completion. The master number 999 demonstrates closure and reflection on something well-done. The three 9s emanate from a common center, mimicking the ancient Celtic symbol called the triskelion. It contains three spirals symbolizing the cycles of birth, life, and death. These three processes remind us to trust in the divine timing of our lives. New beginnings follow endings.

As an important matter comes to a conclusion, you can reflect on what has been achieved or has come to fruition. The power of reflection is embodied by dragonflies, which are a symbol associated with emotional maturity and self-realization.

Angel number 1144

Angel number 1144 reminds you to practice gratitude. In return, you will be showered with abundance and prosperity. Be open to love and light, letting it into your world so that you can reflect it back to others.

Knots are a symbol of abundance. Angel number 1144 is formed from silky, knotted ribbon. Flowers, especially sunflowers, are renowned for their association with gratitude. The number 1 welcomes new intentions, while the number 4 encourages you to ground yourself and cultivate positive processes. The double 1 and double 4 make this number all the more energized and powerful, so harness this passion and project it into your sphere.

Angel number 1234

Ready, set, go! Angel number 1234 is a hugely optimistic sign that you should prepare to receive good news and welcome positive influence into your life. As succulents are thought to attract abundance, so this number is a magnet for good fortune.

Along with gathering energy from the Sun, succulents store water, allowing them to survive and even thrive over dry stretches. Perhaps you have experienced a period of uncertainty or unhappiness? This number could be a sign that difficult times are drawing to a close. The universe is preparing you for an era of spiritual affluence. Let the good times roll!

Angel number 2244

Angel number 2244 is a message of encouragement. Just as a compass guides you in the right direction, seeing the number 2244 reminds you that you have the power and ability to achieve your goals. The combination of the numbers 2 and 4 sends a clear message that action is needed to build security and solidify relationships.

Maintain balance and stability to help you keep on an even trajectory. With the energy of this angel number, you have the power to create the opportunities and life you want for yourself. Just like the animals in this image, be guided by your intuition and you will take the right path.

Mirror numbers, or mirror hours, occur when the clock shows duplicate numbers. It is thought that these numbers point to a divine message, with their unique meaning determined by the specific combination of numbers. They often relate to your deepest desires or emotions.

Mirror number 0909

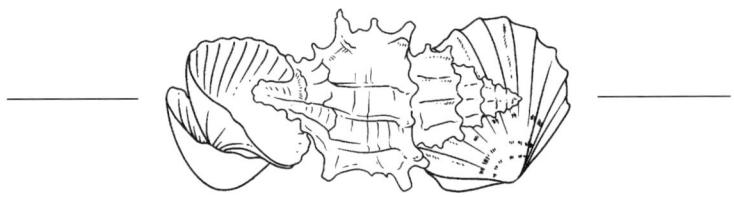

Mirror number 0909 is a sign that the best is yet to come. You are already on a journey of growth, but with this number in your realm, you can feel reassured that the spiritual universe is looking down on you and guiding your path.

Tune in to your inner voice and seek out what no longer serves you. Let go of these things to create space for new beginnings. This will enable you to harness your talents and direct them into areas of your life that you want to enhance. The number 9 represents endings and beginnings, and although one chapter is coming to a close, the next chapter will be more prosperous. Trust in divine timing and reap the rewards of your journey of growth.

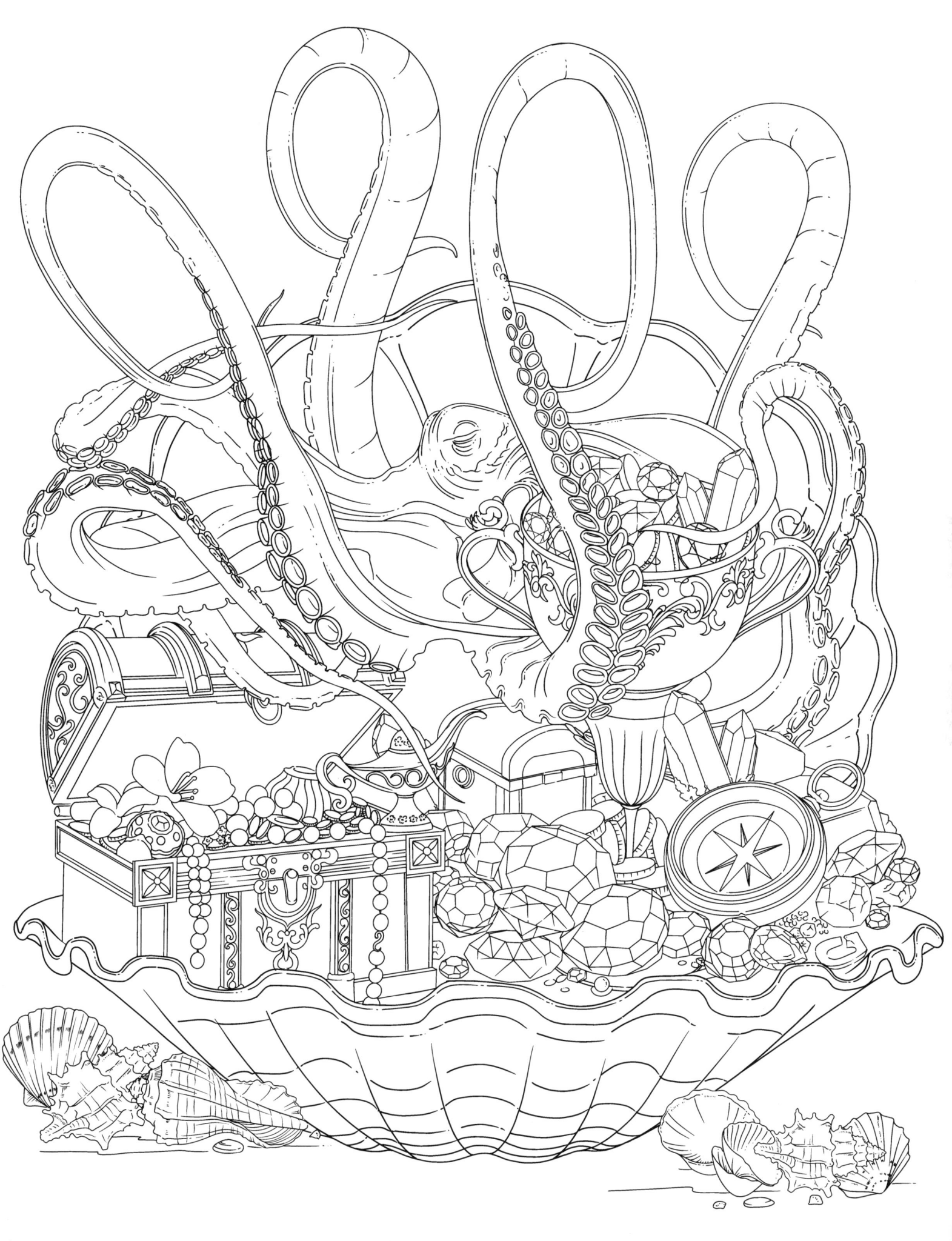

Mirror number 1010

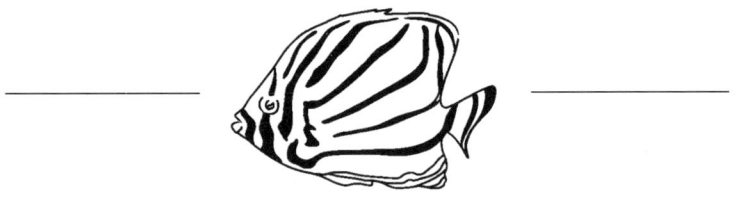

When mirror number 1010 appears frequently, follow your intuition and stay true to yourself. Dive deeply into your pool of self-knowledge and allow yourself to be led by instinct. Just as the noble, intelligent whale navigates treacherous waters using its inner voice, so should you follow your truth.

The universe offers boundless opportunities for those who can tap into their sense of spiritual direction and who practice courage enough to explore this bold new frontier. Mirror number 1010 suggests you are ready to take this step, even if you feel nervous.

Mirror number 1111

The dragon is a protector, symbolizing good luck, fortune, and prosperity. It embraces the meaning of mirror number 1111, which is telling you that everything is in alignment. You are on the right track, with the dragon and the universe as your protectors.

Perhaps you have a hunch about something. If you see 1111, now is your time of power. Seize that opportunity, set your intentions, and manifest heartfelt dreams. It is the right time to be empowered.

The number 1 is associated with new beginnings, with the commencement of journeys, creativity, and leadership. When repeated four times in a row, these qualities are magnified. Take this opportunity to connect to yourself on an elevated level.

Mirror number 1212

If the clock says 12:12, your life choices might have fallen out of time with your intended spiritual path. A frequent sighting of this number can be interpreted as the universe nudging you gently back on track, encouraging you to retreat and reassess your direction.

On a positive note, assessing your choices may offer reassurance that you are heading in the right direction and your plans will come to fruition if you continue along your current path.

Either way, this number asks you to look within yourself. What is working in your favor? What isn't? Be honest with yourself.

In the ancient practice of numerology, all numbers possess a specific energy that can offer insight into a person's individual characteristics. By understanding your unique numerical code, you can better understand who you are, where you're going, and what your purpose is.

Number 0

The number 0 represents the never-ending cycle of life. Change is ahead, but for now, trust in the divine timing beyond your control. You have the power to make your dreams a reality. Even when you hit a low point, the cycle will eventually return you to a high peak. You can manifest your own changes, if you keep moving forward with faith in your infinite cycles—just as the 0 has no beginning or end, your possibilities are endless.

Koi fish swim calmly and peacefully, with their beautiful tails fanning out. Yet hidden beneath this calm demeanor is their perseverance and strength of character. If the universe is showing you the number 0, do not be disheartened by life's challenges. You may feel void or empty, like the blankness of 0, but your time will come.

Number 1

Just as peacocks grow from small brown chicks to magnificently colored birds, you should expand and evolve. The number 1 represents new beginnings and a chance for you to shine. Have the confidence to display your beauty to the world.

As the sun rises on a new day, the number 1 radiates its light on the world and brings hope and the chance to take on life anew. Light creates new life and bestows the energy to start on your journey.

A border of tulips symbolizes the opportunities that await you. Just as bulbs lie dormant in the earth, waiting for their time to spring to life, so can you embrace this opportunity to develop and change.

Number 2

The number 2 is a feminine force, encouraging you to embrace intuitive power. Similarly, lotus flowers, a symbol of female power and hope, rise from muddy waters to bloom and display their magnificence and strength.

Bees demonstrate the peace and partnership of the number 2. In service to the queen bee, they work busily, exuding a feeling of calm efficiency. If you encounter this number, see it as encouragement to work as part of a team, in balance with others, in order to achieve your goals.

Entwined around this number 2 is an endless knot, which, in Buddhism, demonstrates balance. With no beginning or end, it can be followed around forever, displaying the balance needed to empower yourself. This endless renewal is portrayed by peace lilies, as they flourish through the seasons.

Number 3

The powerful symbolism of the number 3 is shown by the necklace the orioles are holding in their beaks. The pendants show the number 3 and the triquetra, an ancient symbol with three interconnecting arcs.

The orioles, which represent the power of friendship, are working together to hold up the necklace, demonstrating the power of social connection. Together we are stronger than the sum of our parts. As a social number, 3 reminds you to make the most of your connections and friendships. Hold each other up and empower one another.

Like the passionflowers that surround the birds, the number 3 symbolizes creativity, imagination, and inspiration. Snapdragons and chrysanthemums denote creativity and optimism. If you encounter this number, let your passions fly and let your loved ones inspire you.

Number 4

Take heed if you see the number 4: You are being reminded by your ancestors that you are supported, safe, and stable. The number 4 is rooted in the ground. It is solid and fixed, and provides a basis for you to grow.

This steady and secure base should give you the power and resources you need to reach for the stars. Aim for the heavens—this number will give you a physical, mental, emotional, and spiritual foundation.

With this number in mind, know that you are being protected and use this divine guidance in whatever way you need. The clean, straight lines of the number will give you the power to seize control and take care of yourself. From this solid foundation grows the tree of life.

Number 5

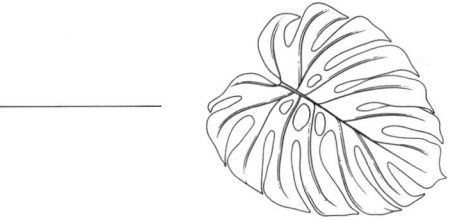

Make like a monkey and tap into your strong sense of curiosity. Like our mischievous primate friends, the number 5 encourages us to embrace a spirit of adventure that can quickly become overshadowed by the practicalities of everyday life. Changing your daily routine could be the simplest way to shake things up and cast off the shackles that may prevent you from living each day to the fullest.

Birds of paradise represent adventure and the beautiful surprises that await when you follow the lead of the number 5. Embrace the twists and turns of life, and learn to go with the flow.

Number 6

The number 6 is linked to the domestic sphere. It embodies the importance of home, shown by the welcoming front door and the steps leading up to it.

The number offers compassion and healing. It provides a place of peace, rest, and security—a snug space for a cat to curl up and have a comfortable nap.

Beautifully scented jasmine and passion-flowers climb up the walls, filling the space with a sense of love and safety, which is also portrayed by the heart-shaped door knocker. The number 6 offers a place of harmony and respite. It promises dependability and domesticity.

Number 7

The number 7 is associated with intellect, introspection, and spiritual depth. It represents a quest for knowledge, wisdom, and understanding. When this number appears, explore the mysteries of life.

7 symbolizes the balance between the conscious and subconscious mind. People who come across this numerological sign are inclined to delve into their inner world, exploring their subconscious to gain insights that might not be apparent. This introspective nature often leads one to become highly intuitive, relying not only on their intellect but also on their gut feelings and spiritual awareness.

The energy of the number 7 encourages a thoughtful, meditative approach to life. It invites individuals to look beyond the surface, integrating intellectual understanding with the wisdom that comes from connecting with their psyche.

Number 8

Renewal and regeneration are the main facets of the number 8. As chameleons can change the color of their skin and adapt to the conditions they experience around them, the number 8 encourages you to make the most of the chances you are given for rebirth and metamorphosis.

Strive for success with the number 8; it is the achiever. Don't be afraid to be goal-oriented. This number symbolizes prosperity, abundance, and material success. Aim high, have faith in your abilities, and make bold choices. The lush, vibrant, and tropical background represents the boundless energy of the number 8.

The chameleons' tails curl together to form the number. Its symmetrical shape reminds you that accompanying this possibility for personal renaissance is a sense of balance. The universe is here to support whatever changes you feel are necessary, so make them with a boldness and braveness of heart.

Number 9

If the universe presents you with the number 9, a cycle is close to fulfillment. This is not the completion. Rather, it is a transition toward your next phase of goals. The number 9 is set inside a coin. The circular shape accentuates this concept of eras—and promises luck and good fortune.

As one circle closes, another opens. This image features two facing phoenixes, which are symbolic of rebirth and transformation. If you encounter the number 9, prepare for new adventures and embrace the challenges in your life, as they will lead to fulfillment.

Lily of the valley, morning glory, and zinnia frame the coin. A fresh start and a new dawn, coupled with the return of happiness, are promised to you by this number.

Master Numbers

Since the birth of numerology, certain numbers are believed to have a turbocharged energy, possessing incredible power and potential. These double-digit numbers harness twice the power of their single-number counterparts. The combined sum of the digits makes them extra special.

Master number 11

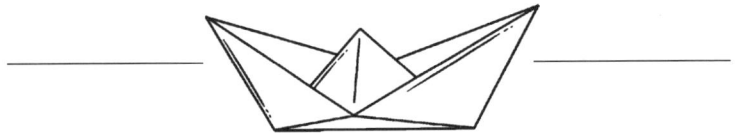

Master number 11 is a powerful symbol associated with spiritual enlightenment and awakening. Two columns rising out of a moonlit pool form the number 11, representing strength. Water, paper boats, and trailing moonflowers symbolize dreams. The number of strength and power emerges.

The reflection of the Moon is seen in the water, surrounded by peacefully bobbing boats and lotus flowers, denoting enlightenment. The number 11 opens up new possibilities for growth, guidance, and insight, guided by the illumination of the Moon.

Dragonflies, a symbol of personal growth, remind us of master number 11's message that out of chaos can come balance, power, and the mastery of one's life purpose.

Master number 22

The duality of the number 2 holds a special place in our collective unconscious. Symbolizing forces such as life and death, yin and yang, or male and female, it represents balance and harmony, as seen in the symmetry of this circular mandala.

The number 2 is peaceful yet powerful, and when the number appears twice as a master number, its force is doubled. Classic feminine traits are displayed by the flowers surrounding the mandala—peace lilies, lavender, and cosmos signify tranquility, and hyacinths embody grace.

Master number 22 is often linked to balance within relationships, merging two individuals' energies into one. It encourages you to strive for internal harmony and find compromise with the forces around you.